M000103910

# Thunderhead

# Thunderhead

Poems

## DAYE PHILLIPPO

*Blessings,*
*Daye Phillippo*

SLANT

THUNDERHEAD
Poems

Copyright © 2020 Daye Phillippo. All rights reserved. Except for brief quotations in
critical publications or reviews, no part of this book may be reproduced in any manner
without prior written permission from the publisher. Write: Permissions, Wipf and
Stock Publishers, 199 W. 8th Ave., Suite 3, Eugene, OR 97401.

Slant
An Imprint of Wipf and Stock Publishers
199 W. 8th Ave., Suite 3
Eugene, OR 97401

www.wipfandstock.com

HARDCOVER ISBN: 978-1-7252-6251-5
PAPERBACK ISBN: 978-1-7252-6250-8
EBOOK ISBN: 978-1-7252-6252-2

*Cataloguing-in-Publication data:*

Names: Phillippo, Daye.

Title: Thunderhead : poems / Daye Phillippo.

Description: Eugene, OR: Slant, 2020. | Includes bibliographical references and
index.

Identifiers: ISBN 978-1-7252-6251-5 (hardcover) | ISBN 978-1-7252-6250-8 (paper-
back) | ISBN 978-1-7252-6252-2 (ebook)

Subjects: LCSH: Poetry. | American poetry -- 21st century. | Country life -- Indiana
-- Poetry.

Classification: PS3566.I6 T48 2020 (print) | PS3566.I6 (ebook)

Manufactured in the U.S.A.                                        JUNE 26, 2020

*In memory of my parents, John and Ola Barkley*

*&*

*With special thanks to Clark Dinwiddie,*
*dear friend and neighbor who welcomed our family to farm country*

Just ask the animals, and they will teach you.
Ask the birds of the sky, and they will tell you.
Speak to the earth, and it will instruct you.

—Job 12: 7—8a

# CONTENTS

## Spring

## AFTER THE GARDEN

*Though your sins are like scarlet, I will make them as white as snow.*
—Isaiah 1:18b

  my sandals were so thick with loam
it was awkward to walk, and lifting each foot
was like walking through deep snow

  like walking through snow, the water
so cold from the hose, pouring over my feet
from the underground river below

  water from the river below washed the loam
from my feet, from the handle and blade of my hoe
here where "loam" rhymes with "poem"

  "loam" rhymes with "poem," though it shouldn't
or should, or couldn't help but, and must, and water
from the Teays, even in August, is so cold,

  so cold from the Teays in August it aches

# Summer

EDGE EFFECT

First day of summer, overcast morning after rain
all night. Lights on in every room. The dripping woods

lean close to the house, so this lamplit room
becomes a room inside a room of trees and weeds,

their leaves, a multitude of shapes and shades of green
and the sky, a close gray ceiling heavy with rain.

When I pass between the lamp's yellow glow
and the window, a young deer, ruddy and feeding

on wild black raspberries at the wood's edge, startles,
leaps through the wall of green, disappears

the way we all hope to pass, one verdant world
into the next, suddenly and with grace.

# (COOL ENOUGH) CIRCA 1975

I sat on the hill under a cantilevered wedge of rock
and surveyed my wilderness, sycamores

and maples, undeveloped scrub a few blocks
from the bus stop. My long hair in the breeze

said I knew how to be free. My blue jeans and
blue chukka boots agreed. I was a pioneer

or a hippie, it didn't matter which. The earth
was under my feet. Someday, I would sleep

in a log cabin, rise at dawn, milk a cow, gather eggs,
plant peas, and walk to the village once a week

where I would encounter books and other folks,
God and watering troughs. On hot days, I would

lean on my hoe, wipe sweat with a frayed blue sleeve,
swig water (cool enough) from a Mason jar,

say, *Ahhhhh!* as I studied the sky, became.

CURRENT

The man who installed our submersible well pump,
lowering it a hundred twenty feet down, said,
"I hear current down there, strong current,"
so I have reason to believe
this water we're drinking is from the Teays,
ancient river, forced underground
when glaciers scrubbed and gritted
their thick Arctic tonnage across this land.
Ponce de Leon searched too far south.
Our ninety-two-year-old neighbor, Clark,
has been coming in thirsty from these fields
for most of his life, splashing his hands and neck,
then slugging down great gulps, wiping his mouth
with the back of his broad, calloused hand,
then kissing his love, his wife, Celena,
sitting down in the kitchen to supper—
fried chicken, buttered potatoes, tomato slices,
green beans from the garden.
For a treat, she'd pop the top
on a jar of zucchini pickles,
his favorite, her specialty. His big hands,
tender on her in her final illness. . . .
Tonight he draws a tall glass of well water.
It stands clear, cold, pure beside his solitary plate
while night comes on, while the Teays
rushes and throbs, while stars appear
in the purpling sky, one by quiet one.

# WEEDING IN AUGUST

Before the day heated up,
before the sun was even up over the big barn,
or the boys had headed off to school,
I went to the garden, started weeding tomatoes,
tufts of tall, wiry grass thrust up
like wild green flames
around the rusted cages. Blades sprung up
from seeds lurking in that bale of dusty straw
I'd found in the barn, and broken open for mulch
to keep the weeds down, I thought.
I ripped it up, tossed it out into the yard.

The sound of those roots being unstitched
from the loose soil, like the sound
of ripping out zipper and seams, again
and again, of that calico mini-skirt, an unlikely green,
I'd stitched in junior high home-ec
until I finally got it right, could wear it,
only it was so short it made my mother gasp
so I couldn't, after all, and the cloth
might as well have been left unbought on the bolt
in the basement sale at Neuwelt's
like weedseedy bales in a barn. Like that.
Like I wish that whatever dark barn and bale
were broken open to release the cancer seeds
sprung up and flaming through
Don and Sam and Betty and Lynette,
had been left untouched, unopened, unspread.

Or wish, at least, that I had hands
that could grasp near its base, tug,
unstitch it from the soft loam
of their bodies,
throw it out into the yard for the mower blade.

# SUMMER DAY

*for John*

When he refused to be born, when he stayed
curled and warm and huge inside, and they
sent me from the hospital saying, *Go home and rest,*
but I weeded the parched garden instead.
After a time, the boy's father stepped outside,
suggested I might come in out of July's brass
for a glass of water, at least, but I glared
until he had to shade his eyes, until he knew
the hundred-degree heat was pumped,
not from the just-past-solstice sun, but from me.
So he gave up, went inside to worry
from the dining room window, instead.
And the birthing never ends.
                              Today, the boy
who took his own good time was drawn from me
again. This time, down our long gravel drive
in a recruiter's car, toward a plane bound
for San Antonio and a DI who will drill
and swear him into that brassy heat.
After the car rolls out of sight, I stumble
to the garden in search of weeds. Weeds
are a mercy—lambsquarters, dock, pigweed,
purslane, butterprint—they give me reasons.
The earth cradles my feet and the sun pours
*hello* and *It'll be okay* over my shoulders
while bobwhites call their names over the pasture,
and the '51 Ford tractor hums and whirrs
along the lane, the profile of the boy's father,
a common comfort as it rides the waves of grass.

# BICYCLING THE BACKROADS AFTER SUPPER

Bicycling the gravel road,
we startle square black calves
in their tall-grass pasture.
Bawling bass voices, the calves
lope, piston-legged
toward their mothers, away
from us wheeling past,
setting sun glinting,
handlebars and spokes,
as if we were ancients or gods
descended
from cow-knows-where
to disrupt the slow bovine evening,
the study of cud.
Our circular motion
must seem peculiar
and suspiciously fluid, our tires
sizzling on the gravel, a meaning
as untranslatable
as Ezekiel's wheel within a wheel,
or the sputter of crop dusters,
or the sounds we make—
chatter and laughter rolling
from our inadequate throats.

# ALGEBRA IS _____ . (FILL IN THE BLANK)

suddenly upon me, like the yellow-green skies of severe weather

the opposite of transcendental

that gray, rust-streaked boxcar inscrutable graffiti tags rattling empty through town

intrusive. My walk to the mailbox has become $-f(x+4) - 2$ with a domain of $[0,4]$

too dangerous to meet at the dining room table while wearing pink pajamas

unlike birds that sing in spring because they've never heard of it

my son's blue, beat-up '89 Buick, repaired, but still less than the reunion of its broken parts

the opposite of wildflowers

a jackhammer in the city of summer

filled with radical signs and my mother warning, "Don't run with sharp objects!"

better than smallpox, the Dust Bowl, or the Johnstown Flood

a clumsy gymnast whapping and flipping around the x-axis suspended between my ears

similar to constellations, but without their romance

not poetry

poetry in the way subtraction can become addition as in the pruning of pear trees

as exponential as "Thirteen Ways of Looking at a Blackbird"

a blackbird caged in the fractal of a leafless pear tree after harvest

blackbird, its bill a less-than sign pointing toward everything not itself

# CENTURIES

*Still, all the history of the world*
*happens at once.*

—"Then Abraham" by Jean Valentine

June in every way—blue sky, sun warming the old earth
the way beautiful young Abishag warms feeble King David.

Birds and breeze, leaves and leafshadow are moving over
the open book and notebook, table where I sit to read.

Adonijah takes Joab and Abiathar into his confidence.
The barn cat, dusty black tabby, curls around my ankles.

Silos across the road. Dried corn, gold rushing, claiming
the grain truck's hold the way Adonijah claims the throne.

A lone orange marigold rises above in its ceramic pot.
*May my lord King David live forever!* exults Bathsheba.

Redwing blackbirds *okalee!* from across the pasture.
A ram's horn is sounding at the spring of Gihon.

Grain truck rumbles away, the next pulls forward. A tiny spider
travels below the counsel of Zadok and Nathan the Prophet.

Solomon is anointed. The earth trembles with the noise of joy.
White yarrow, tall and stately, stirs the air above the deadnettle

the way I stir my tea, turn the page. Centuries pass. (Or don't.)
A man, lame forty years, walks. Peter and John are arrested.

A fat bee browses the spirea. The Sanhedrin interrogates, but
releases the zealots for fear of stirring riot. Squirrels chirr

in the hollow bole of the silver maple. Would I have spoken
or kept silent? Goldflame spirea, bright corymbs of fuchsia.

13

A crow calls from the barnlot, a blue jay from the forest.
An ant walks over *the meeting place shook,*
*and they were all filled with the Holy Spirit.*

1 Kings 1:1–53 & Acts 4:1–37

## INDEPENDENCE

The daylilies' orange fanfare, everywhere along roadsides,
reminding me, story my mother told. Her father, Cecil,

a frugal man, columns of numbers worrying his dark head.
One day, driving his wagon three miles to the grain elevator

in Sedalia for hog feed, his attention was arrested by daylilies
at the roadside, and so he *gee-ed* and *whoa-ed* his team, climbed

down, pulled up a clump—orange ditch lilies in full bloom—
carried them home to his wife and daughter who planted and

watered and watched, not hoping for much, but what they didn't expect
to survive did, and thrived, and the thin, slope-shouldered man

they knew as someone who didn't see beauty in anything other than
worry and numbers that balanced—watery blue ink, Spencerian hand

in a pocket-sized notebook, compliments of Sedalia Grain and Feed—
had to be reconsidered in light of daylilies, and the story told

and retold, summer after summer, each time orange daylilies
came into bloom. Starts of those same flowers, blooming now

by our barn, telling it again—we're all free to do something
other than that which those who know us best expect,

even if only once, even if only daylilies, wild by the roadside.

# BLURRED

Walking out into this morning's milk, sky
and air like something spilled, again, but

not worth crying over. How many more
days of this I can take, I don't know.

Wanting to get in the car, drive until I find
June, blue still up there somewhere behind

this not-fog. Blurred barns and trees, farm
across the road—like old photographs

of themselves, black and white, unfocused.
The curled photograph of my father, young

and on his back in lush grass, one arm
pillowing his head, the other shielding his eyes

from the sun, the look on his face like none I knew.

He's wearing shoes and what appear to be pajamas.
A story here I don't know, even the photograph

not whole, cut down from something larger,
nothing written on the back, like the whole

picture of him I'll never know, but not worth
crying over, any longer. Focusing instead

on today's milk, humidity that holds, concentrates
aromas—old boards, old straw in the old barn

with its hundred-and-a-half years of history.
Milkweed blooming in the pasture, the road's

wet gravel, the brewing storm, even out here
at the mailbox by the road, the coffee brewing

in the kitchen smells close, reminds me to focus
on the picture I knew, my father, good-to-the-last-

drop in his cup, making music on his clarinet
in the back room until arthritis told his fingers *no*.

# PERSPECTIVE

Across three fields and as many roads,
a round white barn and its square white house,
the barn, thimble-sized from here. Above these
the sky going on and on for miles, the way
Winslow Homer in the French countryside, painting
Cernay-la-Ville perhaps *en plein air,* his sky,
summer blue and cumulus, most of the canvas.
Toy-like below, clustered farmhouse and barns.
Foreground, a green field half the size of the sky.
And it's true here, too. This rural landscape
I've been staring at, almost twenty years,
but just today—standing in the art museum,
drawn by the outdoor light in this small painting,
oil on mahogany, 1867, another continent—
learning this about the sky.
How many other ways have I been blind?

# THUNDERHEAD

Last week, at the supper table I was daydreaming
after the meal, looking and not looking
through the dining room's wavy glass,
glass as old as its farmhouse, which is to say
almost a century older than me.
As I'd been doing all afternoon,
I was mulling the word "radiance,"
how to use its Latinate voluptuousness
in a poem in a way that wouldn't seem cheap,
when my husband said, *Your face. It's glowing*,
and I said, *Well, maybe I'll just sit here in this light forever*,
and he said, *No, it's not that.*
*I noticed it earlier, in the kitchen, too.*
At my age, I knew it couldn't be youth, so maybe
the word itself was incandescing? I mean, what if,
in choosing words to ponder we choose
our countenance, too, the simple way
switching out a blackened bulb for new
relights the shade, the room, in which case,
*You have another think coming,*
as my mother was fond of saying, could actually mean
something to look forward to.
The way those thunderheads rolled in
yesterday evening between rains
—white, gray, old lavender rimmed in gold—
cumulus, piled so high they made the sky
into a great Midwestern sea, and thunder
into a great whale sounding its depths,
sights and sounds one might expect
when being born into the next.
The setting sun diffusing gold through
the humid air, light pouring over
beanfield and barn, pasture, cat, every tree

and me, summer robe and flipflops, out
in that light, stepping through wet grass
and the aroma of wet grass, searching,
camera in hand, trying to find a way
to capture it all. Giving up, just standing there,
letting Radiance thunder through my head.

# Autumn

# AUTUMN ORCHARD

Think of it as orchard ladder,
the small argument
of your life, three rails,
narrowing up,
ascended as if above
were loftier, or descended,
as in take you down a rung,
or stepping down, as if
wrestling with angels
were an unholy act
that couldn't
change your name, your nature,
couldn't change you
from supplanter
to contender
with a hip out of joint.
You feel this, to be sure,
the way you feel the spectators'
disapproval. But oh,
how your arches ached
on the rungs!
And your arms, weary,
years up there, balancing
before the dusty grappling.
Your wounded limp back
to the ladder, its tree.
Nevertheless, worth the fruit
not forbidden. Fruit, not
of knowing, but of not
being sick with longing to know.
Ladder, how far up
do your rails travel
before intersecting? But, no.

Here and now, tart-
sweet in the mouth.

## OPEN WINDOW

It is best not to care, too much, or at least, not to state
your case, to wax . . . well, anything. When the day closes
its orange eye in cloudbank, it is best to let sleep

flow in like creekwater around stones, smooth
the day's sharp edges with a sound like chuckling,
as if tomorrow can't help but be better.

Someone will care to hear what you think.
You will wake to the smell of coffee brewing.
You will come down the stairs, and it won't be

descending. After all, your well pump draws
from the Teays. You sip the last Ice Age, and
maybe a sabertooth is just outside, an auk.

You must believe before you can see.
Say a white dove circles a man on his tractor
until he stops, climbs down from mowing,

follows the bird to the house where it lingers,
startlingly white on the roof's black peak. The bird
may only be lost or weary, but if the house is miles

from other houses, and if, while the bird rests,
news is received that the man's mother is gravely ill,
the dove may be something else, too, no matter

who scoffs. Varied sources of light cast innumerable
shadows. Remember feeling certain that nature
recognized you as its own? The scent of autumn

flowing in at the open window reminds you
of that. Time of not feeling the need to explain.
As a child, coming into the house in the evening,

your mother saying, *You smell like outdoors.*

# COYOTE CHAMBER

October's chill dusk and the western horizon
is a persimmon rim, darkening
behind trees. Frost tonight. In dusky light
the woman at the clothesline is pulling cold laundry
from the line, folding the stiff cloth
as much by touch as by sight into a basket.
The dog and cat are with her, too.
Then, coyotes, far off, west. Yips that drift
into something like laughter,
laughter into howl-at-the-rising-moon.
Notes threading through trees like bonfire smoke
through spikes of goldenrod, curling
above the garden's limp-black leavings,
over the mown grass to the clothesline—
five-lined musical staff, post as repeat,
repeat, wooden pin notes.
The cat and dog move close as her cold fingers
fumble-fly at the pins. Yet, when the howls
begin again, she hears more ancient rite
than threat, thinks
chambered cave, flickering firelight,
mineral pigment, no brush. Coyotes singing,
loping the undulating stone.
Chamber of Horses, woman as chamber,
wild notes echoing in her chest.

BREAD

There is a day that comes when you realize
you can't bake enough bread
to make things turn out right, no matter
how many times you read *Little House on the Prairie*
to your children. There aren't enough
quart jars to fill with tomatoes
or translucent slices of pear to keep you
from feeling unproductive. There is no bonfire that burns
orange enough in the chill October night
to keep your mind from following the lonesome
howls and yips of the coyotes concealed
by darkness in the harvested cornfield
just beyond the circle of your fire. And when you
step away from your family and fire,
into the dark pasture and tip your head back,
feel the whole black bowl of sky
with its icy prickles of stars, its swath of Milky Way,
settle over you, you know that no one
and everyone is just this alone on the Earth
though most keep themselves distracted enough
not to notice. In your hollowness
you open your arms to God because no one else
is enough to fill them. Eternity
passes between and no one knows this but you.
The hum of their conversation, the whole world, talking.
When it is time, you turn, grasp the woodcart's handle,
pull it, bumping behind you across the frosty grass,
up the hill to the house, where you
step inside cubes of light, and begin to do ordinary things,
hang up coats, open and close drawers,
rinse hot chocolate from mugs. And you are still
separate, but no longer grieving bread.

# WILD TURKEYS

*After reading Marianne Moore's "The Mind is an Enchanting Thing"*

That morning, eleven wild turkeys,
roaming over the yard and garden
in unison the way my imagination roams,
pecking up the unlikely. The unlikely blue
of the birds' heads and necks long enough to be
a prank played which might have been why
Ben Franklin—pithy wit—lobbied
for them to be the national bird, but big silly birds
that would drown, or so the story's told,
looking up into a hard rain, not majestic.
Figure of this unlikely history
(and Wampanoag and William Bradford, too)
right here in my backyard,
reason I couldn't seem to stop watching
the oddly bobbing heads, stretched-stocking necks,
big black feathers, some sleek, some ragged.
Molted flight feathers like these
carved into quills, nibs dipped into oak gall ink,
put to parchment to pen declaration.
The turkeys, "No kinder to each other than chickens,
probably clutchmates," a friend who knows said.
The pecking order in Constitution Hall,
the free-ranging feather puffing, hiss and throaty gobble. . . .
Eleven wild turkeys roving over my unmown
like history or imagination, like Marianne Moore,
cape and tricorn hat, pen in hand.

# DIORAMA

Almost winter. Saturday evening dusk.
I'm kneading dough
on the enamel-topped kitchen table
when I see deer outside the window.
Framed in the window's long rectangle,
a doe and her yearling, close.

They're cropping grass and weeds.
The doe lifts her head, looks at me.
Her ears ask questions.

*I'm no threat,* I tell her, *My children need to eat, too.*
We go back to what we were doing.

They move around the clearing at sunset
the way I move around the lamplit room.

They aren't the first to graze safely here,
refuge of this backyard,
decades of deer and their offspring.

In my hundred-forty-year-old kitchen,
the table's scarred surface,
women before me, kneading, shaping
dough into sustenance.
Refuge of enough as the sun goes to rest.
          Last glimpse of the deer
before full dark, shadowy shapes
out by the pines.
They stand, watching
the lit window, the diorama there.

# Winter

# CIVILIZING

This is not a black and white photo, this snowy landscape
I stopped my car to photograph on my drive home, though

it appears to be. Fine snow drifting from the open fields
and our road somewhere beneath. In the distance

our big old white farmhouse and barns like tiny boxes placed
on a table covered with white cloth. The treeline beyond

might have been inked by a hand steady as my grandmother's
in her youth—Spencerian script, fractals of the penmanship chart

in her one-room schoolhouse, Hart's Prairie, Illinois, fractals
the way the crowns of trees are fractals of their leaves.

The leaves of the record she kept of the family's wagon trip,
October 1906, Texas to Oklahoma, "Indian Territory"

as it was called then, her stitched sheaf, inscribed, ornate script.
Later, the family moved on again to homestead near Pikes Peak.

A photograph of her with my grandfather on their wedding day,
July 23, 1916, long sleeves in the heat, posing stiffly with a few guests

before a dugout, the people looking small, prairie spreading out
behind them the way these snowy Midwestern fields seem to go on.

I picture her there in winter in that dugout, heart of the earth,
surrounded by the roar of blizzard and the smell of dirt.

Posture-perfect, she sits at a rough table, writing to family
back east, civilizing this wild new life by hand, nib, and ink.

COMMUTER

On my way home after teaching a night class,
driving through lengths of fog like tulle draped

across the highway. Snow-covered farm fields,
highway as history carved into the landscape,

illusion of time traveling fast. Headlights
reflecting back, veil after veil, like years

flashing back, so I wondered what century I'd find
when I arrived at our farmhouse, my silver car

hurtling into the barnyard. Would it stir up time,
chickens and cows bedded down for the night?

Would some startled farmer and wife awakened
by racket, peer down from an upstairs bedroom window

expecting to see a fox at the henhouse, coyotes,
but see me, instead, emerging from my Camry,

dome light flickering, thin music from the radio,
a woman wearing slacks, holding a commuter cup?

# VOYAGER

Outside, the yew clutches slick rockets of ice
and the new snow speaks in shadows, gray-blue.

Inside, the schefflera flutters over the heat register
while the black cat sleuths beneath the bookcase.

Our fifteen-year-old son, e-learning day, travels along,
encapsulated in a starship of living room couch,

isolated pod of brocade soundproofed by ear buds,
the sailing as smooth for him as, before Voyager 1,

interstellar space was thought to be. As smooth
and muffled as I thought parenthood would be

after the children were grown. But shock waves
propagating outward through interstellar medium,

waves crashing charged particles, perturbing plasma,
that dark space between stars. Too soon, this last son

launched—learner's permit, car, job after school.
But for now, "I Can't Turn You Loose" resonating

from his alto sax while schefflera keeps the beat.
Outside, snowflakes, like stars, shuttle to earth.

ELECTION YEAR

In spite of seven below, a blue-bright sky,
so I take my chances with wind, go down

into the woods empty-handed in search of
a poem, but there are none to be found

or there are, and I can't hear, or I
hear, but don't recognize the sound.

Creek, shallow and dull, sluggish with cold,
burble that sounds like drowning. No tracks—

raccoon nor possum—on the slice of icy
shore. No birdsong, no hint of wildflower.

Underfoot, frozen leaf litter, pine cones,
scuffed mud. Overhead, creaks—the arthritic

complaints of trees. On the hill, blasts of cold
are getting under even the patient old barn's skin,

doors slamming, threatening to unhinge.

## ABRAHAM TREES

Gangle-shanked winter trees lurch,
gaunt against the death rattle wind.
Stripped of thousand-leaf voices,
they creak on cold, arthritic knees
drained of innocence. Severed limbs,
the long list of battle-dead.
Like Lincoln shambling toward Gettysburg,
a few brief words scratched on a scrap
tucked in his tophat, their weight
heavy, so heavy, on his disheveled head.
*That speech won't scour,* he said afterwards,
but of course it did, and lived,
perennial, like he and the trees,
scouring the earth with their roots,
sheltering a nation beneath their leafy heads.

## AT LINCOLN'S HOME IN SPRINGFIELD

I bent over the glass display case
and stifled a chuckle at what a curator
had considered relic enough to encase, elevate
on a white pedestal—
a brown, tiger-eye swirl porcelain doorknob
exactly like the doorknobs
we use every day
in our hundred-fifty-year-old farmhouse
one state east.
Ridiculous, I thought
such a common object on display
and then thought of the hand,
long-fingered and burdened, that had turned it.

# MAP

Snow curling the dirt road like chalk dust
as if wind were erasure, a school of thought.

Paint I began scraping, small curl, back
of the bathroom door, peel I'd planned

to scrape, sand, retouch. Small project
become one-thing-after-another, layer

after layer, irregular as treaties with tribes,
cessations, wilderness owned by no one

now bisected by lies and lines, waterways as
boundaries. Map of peeling paint, this door

—blue, sepia, Dover, old rose, sea green,
and beneath, shellac over pine—1865

when the door opened to stairwell, wedged treads
turning a sharp degree, upward curl that led

to servant's quarters, small room separated
from the family's rooms by a closet, double-

walled. Stairwell of wondering who, serviceable
shoes, creased and dusty, run-over at the heels,

had gathered her weariness and faded skirt
for the cold steep climb of years, of dream.

## SOON, SPRING

Snow is falling softly past the windows, no wind to drive it,
so the flakes take their time, turning, some rising a bit again

like the clouds of gnats one sees stirring by the roadside in fall.
Mother Goose preening her feathers, my father used to say

of snow like this, snow intending no harm, not blinding drivers
or the woman walking out to her mailbox on its leaning post

by the gravel road. Motherly snow, gently blanketing the garden
and house, fences and fenceposts, giving the mailbox a little

peaked cap. Blanketing also, one supposes, the white-tailed deer
we haven't seen by the white pines for days now. Herd of nine

at last count, frisky among the fragrant, soft-needled branches,
then loping off downhill to the creek, trail into the deep woods

where I imagine them snuggled, nose to tail, sheltered together,
next spring's fawns warm and sprouting in their bellies, fawns

waiting the way wildflowers wait to be called into the world, the way
our grandson waits, curled in his mother's belly. Soon, spring!

## EN POINTE

Under the neighbor's boxwood, I see what their dog
has dragged up out of the woods, a deer's severed foreleg,

and when I say under, I mean almost, but in plain view
near the front porch, and when I say neighbor, I mean

two-and-a-half miles and my daughter-in-law's parents
where I'm dropping off our three-year-old granddaughter

so she can catch a ride to ballet class, and by boxwood,
I mean hedge, evergreen, leaves opposite, lanceolate

and leathery, but in winter not, thank goodness, odor
of cat urine. Boxwood boxing in the sidewalk as precisely

as if we were in Cheshire instead of the Midwest, and when
I say dog, I mean border collie named Fly, strong smell

of skunk when she greets us, and when I say greets,
I mean friendlier than I want from a skunk-smell dog,

and when I say woods, I mean, all around, primitive thicket,
and when I say deer, I mean young, and my granddaughter

looking on. By severed I mean, at the top, white, gnarled joint,
grisly string of ligament, and by foreleg, I mean, ruddy fur

intact down to delicate black hoof, tapered, *en pointe* forever.

## TO THE ANGEL IN MY LIVING ROOM

Angel above the closet door, prone
in flight among stars, trumpet to lip,
long white gown and chestnut hair flowing,
ribbon of old rose trailing beneath you
so as not to become entangled in wings.
Framed in half-opened eye, framed
in plastered transom, you sail motionless
(though suggestive of motion) above history,
the door's creaky hinge, closet beneath
the stairs, space reducing back like years,
items stored in there changing over time, now
my vacuum sweeper, cans of paint,
old Super 8 movie projector and reels,
our children still babies just being born,
just learning to walk. But in 1865, back
when this house was built? Broomcorn
broom, black metal dustpan? Curling scraps
of leftover flowered wallpaper, shellac
for woodwork and floors, a tintype or two?
Angel who guards the door, musician
of music I cannot hear, musician who appears
to be looking away, what do you think
of our comings and goings, our various notes
and dramas? Or perhaps it's not for you to say.
Your clarion call to mystery, not terrifying
like visitations by biblical counterparts.
I don't tremble or faint in your presence,
in fact, most often I forget you're up there
as any dustcloth would show. Perhaps your
lyric goes something like this: Forgetting

is a layer of dust, a half-opened eye,
a plastered transom in which to be suspended
at the door of dark space going back
years, while memory is a mote, an anthem,
old rose that may entangle if one forgets
to drape it out of the way of wings.

PRAYER

December in Michigan, hospital parking lot, cars
humpbacked with new snow, people sled-footed,

slow barges slipping toward this or that port.
Commerce of change. Yesterday, our daughter,

seven months pregnant, ruptured appendix,
the surgeon's hands sliding in, near the womb.

Today, IVs in each arm, their alarms.
Needles and vials, charts. Nurses in and out

on whispering shoes. I walk out to the car
for a book and to move, breathe weather.

A young woman just arrived bears a gift
wrapped in blue, a mylar balloon floats over

like fair weather. She smiles up at the windows.
A middle-aged man looking down, hurries past

wrapped into himself, his heavy coat, his news.
By the walkway, a rose garden. Spent leaves,

thorny canes pruned back against freeze, but
one deep-pink blossom spared, snow lodged

between petals. Blossom in winter, declaring.

# A VISIT TO MY DAUGHTER IN CHARLEVOIX

I walk out of the warm house in order not to hear words,
to think my own storms, falling barometric pressures.
In the house, four grandchildren—a flurry of hands

and feet, kisses and questions—all-consuming weather.
Sand edges the narrow blacktop that edges Susan Lake.
The wet sand grits beneath my steps.

Mailboxes, loaf-shaped, bear unfamiliar names.
The houses seem random—a barn, a trailer,
a bungalow and cabins, a landscaped fieldstone—

as if the zoning board forgot to convene, or were
undecided. But no matter, the neighbors are good.
At the boat access, the thick feel of sand dragging

at my shoes is pleasant as I walk down to the water.
Anything out of the ordinary can be joy. I sit
on a cold boulder, listen until, slowly, faraway sounds

—a train horn, dogs, traffic on the highway, a crow
across the lake—make their way to me, but keep
their distance. Their reticence becomes a silence.

Wind ripples the dull gray water to the shore
in arcs. Reeds intercept the arcs, translate
them into crosshatches, until the face of the lake

resembles an old woman's face, lined with time
and wisdom. She knows that only a few worries
actually come true, lap at the rocky overhang

of life. Most are absorbed by the shore, never
needing to have been thought. Water continues,
does not cry out, anguished, from the sand.

I nudge out the shells of three freshwater snails.
White, tiny as baby teeth, yet empty, translucent.
With one finger, I roll them in my palm, these

houses curled like question marks. Whole lives
lived in there . . . I rise, tip the shells, weightless,
into my pocket. They nestle together in the seam.

# GREAT LAKES

*for Caleb*

At fifteen, he stands blond and lanky,
gazing out the louvered hospital window
onto a Lake Michigan
as green and chopped as slag glass,
fracture lines curving each wave.
With his parents, he traveled north
to meet their newest grandson,
the boy's nephew. The baby,
early in utero a twin, but born alone.
*Never* is its own weeping.

On the drive up, the call.
Their ninety-six-year-old neighbor, Clark,
the boy's best friend,
the boy's "ninety-six-year-old teenager,"
the boy's "I wanted him to be my best man," born
into the next life.

In the room's dim light, a grief as green
as the winter lake settles over the boy.
If only the waves could draw it
like the wreckage of six thousand ships,
out into the lake's great heart.

# Spring

## DECIDUOUS

Early March, early evening.
In a scrimmy sky,
the sun's pale jonquil
has allowed herself, for a moment,
to rest, in a net
of leafless dendrites,
round crown of a sugar maple.
Best time of year.
Time when deep winter
has spun open its vise,
yet one can still see every
branch, every bud, every bird
the trees are thinking.

# AN APRIL NOMENCLATURE

*Quis nomen tuus est?*

Cast the blue-flowered cape about your shoulders
for a breezy midday ramble. When the wind fingers
the cape's fringes, call yourself Woman with Wings.

Instead of the gravel lane, travel the unmown field.
Call yourself Woman who Walks on Wild Violets,
Woman Who Treads Galaxies of Dandelion Suns.

When you pass the burn pile's tangle of branches, and
worry that the pair of robins you see there are nesting,
call yourself Queen of Birds and decree they move on.

Inform the cheeky fox squirrels chuckling down at you
that you are the distinguished Professor of Laundering.
Point out adherents to your theories waving wildly

from the clothesline. Call the Wind your friend. When you
see that the raspberry cane you bought (almost nothing)
at a Mennonite woman's sale, has overtaken the garden,

call yourself Entrepreneur, Farmer of Pies and Jams.
The pear trees, call them sisters. Put your heads together,
whisper secrets about bees and deer. When the woes

of your grown children and grandchildren and friends
attempt to tag along, grant them wings and wind.
Wave a wildflower scepter. Decree peace, Sovereign

of Solitude. When you step into the white pine cathedral,
its carpet of duff (this hush), look up through the Sistine
of needles at cloud and aquamarine, call yourself Humbled

By Everything. And Woman with Wings, when vultures
circle darkly, show them *your* wingspan, tell them *your* names.
Tell them again. Remind them you are the Wind's.

# THE EXTENT OF PASSION

The school board non-renewed the contract
of the first-year English teacher,
though he had developed rapport
with his students, excited them about Shakespeare,
because he couldn't coach football.
Instead of, "Goodnight, Sweet Prince,"
the tombstones of future Fountain County
generations will read, "Go, Ramblers!"
And that will be the extent of passion.
And yet, I'm loath to leave because
I wandered an urban wilderness
for forty years before moving to Beulah Road,
and my eighth child, fifth son, Noah, was born upstairs
seven years ago tomorrow in the southeast bedroom
on a rainy Sunday afternoon in May.
And because my ninety-one-year-old, neighbor, Clark,
who told me about first laying eyes on the woman
he would marry when she was picking tomatoes in a field,
has instructed me in all the law and the prophets
by loving his God and his neighbor as himself.
And for the sake of the barn swallows that orbit
in evening light above the new-mown grass,
gorging themselves in a thick mote of mosquitoes,
and for the Little Shawnee River that tells me
the current would have no voice without
rocks and bends and shallows,
and for the black locust trees that envelop me
in white fragrance as I stand beneath
the rough, wicked-twisted branches
in a rain of tiny perfect petals.

# BREATHING IN

*for Noah*

In the night, she breathes in the fragrance
of sun and breeze, basket of line-dried sheets
as if the fibers had memorized the day—

fair-weather clouds, bees-at-white-clover,
variegated hosta, birdsong, robin's-egg-blue.
White paint peels from the old garage

the way bark peels from the old silver maple
near the house, tree that tossed in the wind
one rainy Sunday afternoon in May

while she labored, stormy ebb and flow
of the body soothed by the ebb and flow
of leaves. The boy born that day, youngest

of eight, a teenager today. His father's hair now,
white as a sun-dried sheet. His mother, awake
in the dark, knowing what a basket knows,

carry and hold, how time-lapse goes a day.

# ORDINARY GHAZAL

I will seek a letter at the mailbox's red flag, how many more times?
Walk this puddled gravel drive with the dog and cat, how many more times?

Dislike the sight, row of brown molehills risen like my own petty complaints?
Be here to hear the just-before-spring birds tune up, how many more times?

My life, ordinary as unmown grass, tattered and dormant in fencerows. . . .
Sons asleep upstairs under quilts pieced of castoff jeans, how many more times?

Witness sunrise over the barn, frost on the grass, deer by the pines? Think of
Jesus asking that man, *Do you want to be made well?* How many more times?

Think of Him asking me. Of walking back to the mailbox in late afternoon,
of pulling it open, reaching in, again, how many more times?

# BARBED WIRE POEM FOR TWO VOICES IN TIME DELAY

A woman of a certain age should not attempt to climb over a barbed wire fence
 *In Purdue's Elliot Hall of Music, Skillet's, Korey Cooper, clad in skin-tight black,*
no matter how much she is intrigued by that half-submerged stone in the creek,
 *explodes onto the stage like a first responder at a trauma scene. She wields*
even if the stone might be a gravestone washed down from the graveyard uphill.
 *her gleaming white rhythm guitar like a tool designed for specialized rescue.*
The woman should not climb the fence. She should walk the fenceline, search for a gap
 *In thrall, the audience begs to be set free from their ordinary lives, transported.*
and if there is no gap, she should search for a gate. Then search again.
 *In black, spike-heeled boots, Ms. Skillet skip-kicks herself to the back of the stage*
In lieu of gap or gate, the woman searches for a place the fence sags. Just enough.
 *then races toward the pleading, screaming crowd, leaps*
In this way, she will be able to press—wire between barbs with one hand—then lean
 *into the pyrotechnic air, all while throbbing a barrage of notes,*
on her walking stick, shift her balance and lift one rusty-hinged leg over
 *then lands on her flexible young knees, slides*
the barbed wire. But she must have chosen her stick wisely. It must not snap.
 *to the precipice of the stage,*
When it snaps, she must not pull away. But when she does, she must quickly perceive
 *without missing even one hot-wired beat.*
that it is not only her ruined favorite jeans that are hooked, but also one of her two
 *Invincible, she leaps to her feet, rhythms more rescue*
favorite legs, tender inner thigh impaled on a rusty barb like a shrike's next meal.
 *while her head snaps forward and back and her black hair screams*
The woman is alone in the silent woods, except for the dog who will tell no one.
 *forward and back as the metal continues to pulse from her arms.*
It is a soft pre-spring afternoon, the creek melodious as bird song. Glory-of-the-snow
 *At the concert, watching from the precipice of the balcony*
stirs, blue beneath the loam. The woman, who curiously does not feel alone, prays,
 *the woman decides that she wants a medical i.d. tag which states that*
O! Rescuer of All Those Entangled, Holy Extractor of Every Rusted Barb,
 *if she is ever in need of defibrillation,*
I beseech you, teach these fingers to see the way free. Barbs must come out

*Korey Cooper's music is the machine she wishes to have applied.*
along the same jagged path. The woman's palm is bruised from pressing the wire
*Despite her bruised palms and graying hair, the woman claps like a fangirl,*
while her unseeing fingers fumble their way to releasing the cloth, then finally the leg.
*stamps her wounded leg in time with the remedy*
She limps up the hill, thinking about tonight's concert, tries not to think
*while she considers whether, after the concert, she should*
of tetanus, or tick fever, or that possible tombstone in the creek.
*consider a future in assisted living or take up aerobic guitar.*

## YOU FALL INTO IT

That ink stain
shaped like Kentucky
on your great-grandfather Orpheus's library table
at which you now sit to translate Hebrew.
You wonder what he would think, this ancestor,
"Beloved Country Minister" his gravestone reads,
born a hundred years before you
in a time when it was expected that a woman
would pore only over *Godey's Lady's Book*,
*I know you will pardon my long silence,*
*when you learn the important fact that I am at housekeeping,*
or receipts clipped from newspapers,
add butter the size of a walnut.
Housekeeping as holy writ, butter as The Way.

His twenty years of writing sermons.
His wife, Mary, in the kitchen
creaming butter and sugar by hand
with a green-handled wire whip, blue bowl
tucked firmly against her side.
The inkspill.
What caused it? Epiphany or distraction?
The Man called Jesus, or a scarlet bird
perched in the boxelder just outside
the study window, its *what cheer-cheer-cheer*?
And Orpheus, did he call out to Mary?
Did she step out of the kitchen?

## MOTH

Malpighi's discovery of periodic reversal of direction in the heart-beat . . . has remained almost in oblivion for nearly 260 years. Réaumur held that in the pupa and adult moth the heart beats backward; in the caterpillar, forward.

—*History of the Discovery of Periodic Reversal of Heart Beat in Insects*, John H. Gerould, 1933

If your great-grandfather's name was Orpheus,
and your grandfather's, Cecil, it seems only natural

to long for music and second sight, a paisley
like a female Promethea's wing. Why all this art

when her dark mate finds her, not by sight,
but by pheromone in moonlight? Who can say . . .

Along the curved margins of her wings,
—color of old parchment—stitches of flame,

but this moth is not drawn to flame. Apex
of each forewing, dark eyespots initiating

mysteries as they loom, wide, blind stare.
Capsule of her head, a pair of ferny frons,

a thick crop of burgundy "hair," wild as any rocker's
before a concert of screams.
        But silence along the moth's hindwings,
inner margins, feathery scales that draw the eye

yet conceal the striped lozenge of her body.
In the same way, the burgundy covers of the book

—poems Orpheus's sister, Arcella wrote, 1874—
conceal the lines and old parchment of many elegies.

This friend lost to settle the west, that one to war,
another to childbed. Arcella, too, gone

before she was thirty. Sad, ancestral music unlike
my children's music that used to flow

from the open windows of our house
—piano, flute, guitar, djembe, saxophone—

and wrap itself around me in the garden softly,
so that pulling weeds became

Moonlight Sonata, Be Thou My Vision, My All in All,
heartbeat, Gonna Fly Now.
                              Promethea caterpillar

in autumn, silks wild cherry leaf to stem, folds the leaf close
as she spins herself within,
                              waits, suspended until

with a slow, backward beating of her heart, she ecloses
into flight, into elegy, spring's burgundy flame.

# MYSTERY

We all believe in mystery. The way one thing becomes another
  because we say it does, but only if it's true.

The way the male red-wing blackbird, royal red epaulets,
  makes of a grass stem a dais, the way he *ok-a-lees!*

The way starling rabble on the lawn mimic and mock.
  The way the striped gray tomcat, after his roam, comes home cold,

with a puffed tail, forgets (or remembers) like a teenage son, begs
  to be let out again. The way the yellow crocus, the lavender crocus, yawn awake,

lazy at the woods' edge, in the same way the watch dog, lazy at the garage,
  welcomes home a stranger like family because his spirit

tells her this is true. The way white pines and red pines
  are so adamantly green and do not envy the way a crushed white fir needle

releases the fragrance of tangerine. The way a cardinal's
  *what-cheer-cheer-cheer* becomes my mother's laughter.

Thin white scar she bore on her hand, record of a day in her twelfth year
  when she rescued a meadowlark from a cat's jaws, the way this gave

birds and mercy precedence. And the cottonwood twig she planted
  as a child by the water trough on their dry-grit pinto bean homestead, the way

it rooted and thrived while her father's store-bought saplings died. The way
  words take root. A scene in Genesis, shepherds gathered at a desert well.

Flocks of parched sheep, bleating heat of the day. The dust and din.
  Then Rachel, with her flock. The way translating this verse—Jacob,

the way he greeted her with a kiss—bewildered me with sudden tears
  before I knew the next words, and he lifted his voice and he cried out.

The way watered and kissed in Hebrew sound so much the same. The way I knew that moment, that day, by the way its dove fluttered through my ribcage.

KEEPING TIME

Driving up Fourth Street hill after seven yesterday evening, apricot sky,
little traffic,
I passed the exact spot where Daddy and I traveled (another line in time)
in his blue Ford pickup with the topper—paint cans and brushes,
speckled ladders and drop cloths, hawk and trowel, plaster and trough—
even the cab of the truck smelling damp with these.
In this spot, as an adolescent, I saw him use the rearview mirror
to flip off a tailgater, and was shocked.
I mean, church and Sunday school! Every week, all of us,
but in the summer, not my father
when he dropped us off, then went to rehearse,
Lafayette Citizens' Band, so we caught a ride home
with Brother and Sister Nichols, the stuffy black sedan
of their disapproval of his "lapse"
making me feel pitied and slightly ashamed.
My father, blue eyes, dark hair slicked back with Vitalis, clarinet to his lips.
The way he played "Hello, Dolly!" and "The Holy City,"
equal fervor. We knew he was wild.
He liked mustard. And pepper! And sometimes ate salami.
It was more than we could understand.
Maybe leaving home when he was fourteen?
Or hitchhiking to Indiana, change jangling in his pocket?
Maybe his years with the Barnum & Bailey band . . .
red and white big top, town after town. Set up, tear down,
every day, the piquant smell of sawdust
and elephants and moving on. What does one talk about
with coworkers who tame tigers or fly on a trapeze?
Sequined ladies, ostrich feathers waving from their headbands,
gracefully walking on balls, a feat I tried once when I was five,
but fell from that less than astonishing height,
broke my arm. My first hint that I would never be glamorous
or transient or suspended.
Rooted here, only one county south of where I grew up,

64

never meeting even one member of my father's family.
This mystery. Oh, he floats through the air with the greatest . . . .
In our small, Third Street living room, a console radio—
cherry case, doors thrown open to reveal the RCA logo,
a white dog listening intently to "His Master's Voice"
at the horn of a gramophone, a soft, yellow glow behind the dial,
the smooth, weighted feel of the tuning knob,
the soft hum of tubes as they warmed . . . the way the music
would fade in like memory . . . . My father in his wingback chair,
eyes closed as he listened intently
to the music, his legs crossed, one foot suspended
and swiveling at the ankle, keeping time.

# FLEDGLING

The dwarfism community has voiced that they prefer to be referred to as
dwarfs, little people, people of short stature or having dwarfism, or simply,
and most preferably, by their given name.

—*"The 'M'Word," Little People of America website*

Robin fledgling, so still in the garden's
deep shade, your colors
are like earth and sunlight sieved
through leaves.
You are shrugged into yourself,
even your dark round eye, not
blinking, all of you saying,
Not here, not here, not here
in a language so quiet
it makes you noticeable,
unnoticeable, says,
               girl I once was
adolescent walking out of the nest
out ahead of the rest
—grandmother, mother, brother—
their short limbs making them seem
"too slow," I thought
when some kid riding toward me
on a bike, called out, pointing,
"Did you see that family of midgets
behind you?" then snickered and rode off
leaving me glad, not glad, noticeable,
unnoticeable in a way they
could never be
just the ordinary play of light
and shadow, sidewalk or garden floor.

# GOING ABOUT THE HOUSE

Our cheerful, little dark-haired mother
in that pint-size 1950s bungalow.

In the picture window, a white metal shelf
pressed its elbows casually to the plaster.

On the shelf, rust bubbled in circles
beneath clay pots of African violets.

The long-necked watering pot, spout
she tipped, just enough, to let water

gurgle out. The violets' leaves, robust,
fleshy and finely-haired, and at the whorled

heart of each plant, a profusion of blossoms
—white, pink, purple, lavender—single- or
double-petaled, double-crochet ruffles

like the doilies her mother crocheted.
Beyond the window, a square

of clipped grass, a birdbath's shallow twinkle
in which robins flickered their wings

spraying a radiance of droplets, sunlit
at the whorled heart of memory. Sunlight

and birds and African violet blossoms,
echoes of our mother's voice—alto

when spoken, but soprano when singing softly
as she tended violets, went about the house.

# POUR

In the night, wind and rain poured down the chimney,
a reverse smoke. In every room, the smell of wet ashes.

I walk toward the woods carrying the milk glass vase
of spent iris. The air is electric and blue with wind.

Stacks of black clouds race, skewing light and shadow.
Strange light where memory finds you, bearing the weight

of your mother's vase—her hands, her wedding band.
From the yew, a sparrow whirrs, suddenly, rising

the way woodsmoke rose from the chimney all winter.
But today, memory, rain's reverse smoke.

# AT FOURTEEN

One afternoon, I was sitting cross-legged
on the kitchen linoleum, cracking black walnuts
for something to do. Cast iron mortar, pestle,
little four-posted castle, little jagged scatter
of shells on the floor, nutmeats in a blue bowl.

My doll-sized grandmother was perched
on a red dinette chair, her feet not reaching
the floor. The chair's chrome legs,
bent at the knees like prayer.

I felt her eyes on me.  So rare.

Brindled light it must have been that filtered down
through the crochet of houseplants
on the windowsill over the sink, doily of light
that rested on my head.

*You have pretty hair, the sun on it like that*, she said,
her old voice wavery as water
from a downspout after rain. Praise!
Gift she'd never before given.
Then, *My hair used to be that color, too,*
took it back again.

DECORATING THE GRAVES

Cemetery on a hill, Geetingsville.
Wind whipping our hair and clothes, carrying words off
over the rolling farm fields
just beginning to bristle with corn leaves,
green penmanship neat as a careful child's
precise lines. Memorial Day and
my middle-aged brother and middle-aged me
are doing one of the few things
we still do, just us two,
decorating the graves—parents, grandparents,
great-grandparents, great uncles and aunts,
an infant second cousin, 1926,
another, a girl of twelve, 1931. Children
of Edith and Robert, whom we never knew.
Such grief before antibiotics,
before our time, a grief we never knew
the way we never knew
the heft of the black hand pump standing,
top of the hill against the sky.
Never knew what it was to wrestle
the iron handle up
and down like a strong man's arm.
Never knew priming the pump, waiting
for water to splash out.
Water on tap, what we knew.
The flowers we've brought, made in China.
They'll bloom all summer and fall, winter too,
and next May, will hopefully (like us),
though faded and frayed, be blooming still,
only a few petals torn away.

## GEESE

This morning, I walked out through the wet unmown
to listen to my husband's bees, hive
behind the back pasture, new to us this spring.

Geese beagling their approach. I looked up
as the pair emerged, side by side, into full view
just over the black locusts. Heavy birds, flying

so low you could almost feel the weight
of their bodies in the lift and fall of their great wings,
moving as if in slow motion.

Low, over the white pines, so low it seemed
the needles must brush their breasts, and talking
in honks, syllables of dactyl and spondee intermingled,

so that one heard them inseparably in what seemed
agreeable discussion about bodies of water
(so many this year) and nesting places, or perhaps

hopes for this year's goslings, number and trait.
Do they anticipate?  Only they and God know . . . .
This coupling through the chill air, this

solemn drink offering poured out over the morning
and the woman below.

# GREAT CRESTED FLYCATCHER

*Peterson's Field Guide to the Birds East of the Rockies*

We were quiddling away our Sunday afternoon
at cards when we heard it, a bird's loud whistle,
close, right at the dining room door. On the step

where the barn cat rests, a single bird, cinnamon tail,
gray wings and crest, yellow on its breast, black bill.
For so long, the same old cards, the same old

sparrows, then this for which we had no name.
*Wheeep!* that woke us from our sleep, then turned
to catch my eye, then flew away.

# ACKNOWLEDGMENTS

With gratitude to the editors of the publications in which these poems first appeared.

*Adirondack Review*

*The Cape Rock*

*The Chariton Review*

*Cider Press Review*

*Crux*

*The Exponent*

*Foliate Oak*

*The Fourth River*

*Great Lakes Review*

*Lindenwood Review*

*Lines + Stars*

*Literary Mama*

*Mad River Review*

*MERVOX Mom Egg Review*

*Mothers Always Write*

*Natural Bridge*

*North Central Review*

*Northwest Indiana Literary Journal*

*Off the Coast*

*Presence*

*Relief*

*RipRap*

*San Pedro River Review*

*Shenandoah*

*South Carolina Review*

*THEMA*

*Valparaiso Poetry Review*

*The Windhover*

Jean Valentine, "Then Abraham" from *Break the Glass*. Copyright © 2010 by Jean Valentine. Reprinted with the permission of The Permissions Company, LLC on behalf of Copper Canyon Press,

www.coppercanyonpress.org.

All quotations from the *Holy Bible* are from the *One Year Bible* New Living Translation.

This book was set Perpetua, designed by the British sculptor, artist, and typographer, Eric Gill, in response to a commission in 1925 from Stanley Morrison, an influential historian of typography and adviser to the Monotype foundry. The design for Perpetua grew out of Gill's experience as a stonecarver and the name pays tribute to the early Christian martyr, Vibia Perpetua.

This book was designed by Shannon Carter, Ian Creeger, and Gregory Wolfe. It was published in hardcover, paperback, and electronic formats by Wipf and Stock Publishers, Eugene, Oregon.

CPSIA information can be obtained
at www.ICGtesting.com
Printed in the USA
BVHW030028290720
584592BV00004B/23